O

BURGMÜLLER-SCHAUM

18 STUDIES, OPUS 109

The Purpose of the Burgmüller-Schaum Edition

Johann Friedrich Burgmüller (1806–1874) was a German composer known primarily for his piano music. Settling in Paris as an adult, he adopted a light style to satisfy the demand of Parisian music lovers and wrote numerous pieces of salon music for piano. He also published several albums of piano studies that have become standard works. *18 Studies, Op. 109* addresses a variety of technical problems. Although classified as études, Burgmüller effectively links technical problems with appropriate musical ideas to create what are, in essence, character pieces. Mr. Schaum has renamed some of the exercises with appealing titles that more accurately reflect the mood of the piece. Special emphasis is placed on equal development of both hands, and technical points are equally divided between the right and the left hands. Some of the exercises are purposely abridged, thereby avoiding stiffness and tension. Exercises given in their original form include editorial fingering and pedal indications. Using the **Burgmüller-Schaum** exercises will improve piano technic when used in conjunction with a program of balanced piano repertoire. **Burgmüller-Schaum** is a valuable sourcebook for sight reading, for technical development, and for growth in musicianship.

Editor: Gail Lew
Production Coordinator: Sharon Marlow
Cover Illustration: Magdi Rodríguez
Cover Design: María A. Chenique

Contents

Quiet Stream (Op. 109, No. 1) 4

String of Pearls (Op. 109, No. 2) 6

Ice Regatta (Op. 109, No. 3) 3

The Gypsies (Op. 109, No. 4) 8

Springtime (Op. 109, No. 5) 10

Jumping Rope (Op. 109, No. 6) 12

Sailing (Op. 109, No. 7) 14

The Restless Molecule (Op. 109, No. 8) 16

Church Bells (Op. 109, No. 9) 18

Snow Flurries (Op. 109, No. 10) 20

Patio Dancing (Op. 109, No. 11) 26

Dog Trot (Op. 109, No. 12) 23

Thunder Storm (Op. 109, No. 13) 28

The Gondolier's Song (Op. 109, No. 14) 31

Acrobatic Dancer (Op. 109, No. 15) 32

Undertow (Op. 109, No. 16) 35

March (Op. 109, No. 17) 38

The Spinning Top (Op. 100, No. 18) 40

ICE REGATTA

Contrasting legato and staccato

Op. 109, No. 3

QUIET STREAM

Finger legato

Op. 109, No. 1

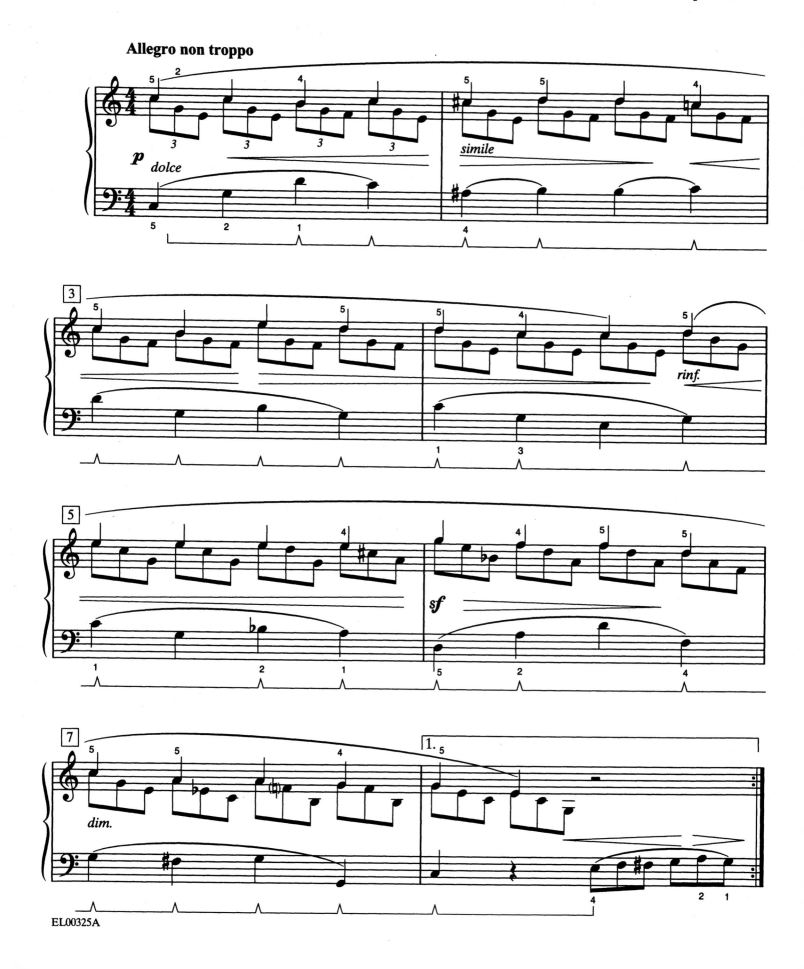

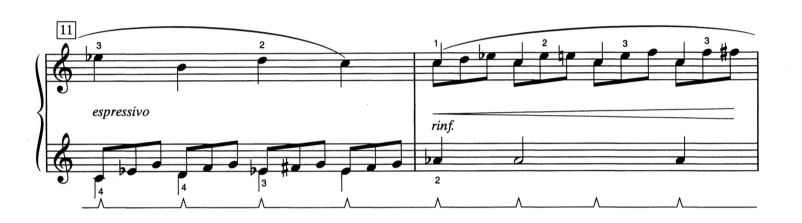

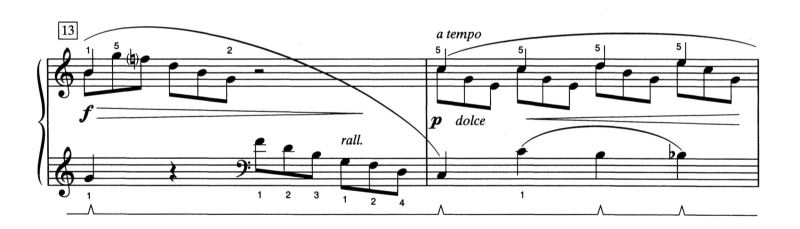

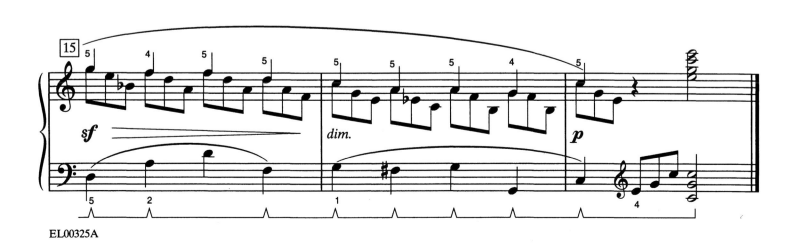

STRING OF PEARLS

Scale passages

Op. 109, No. 2

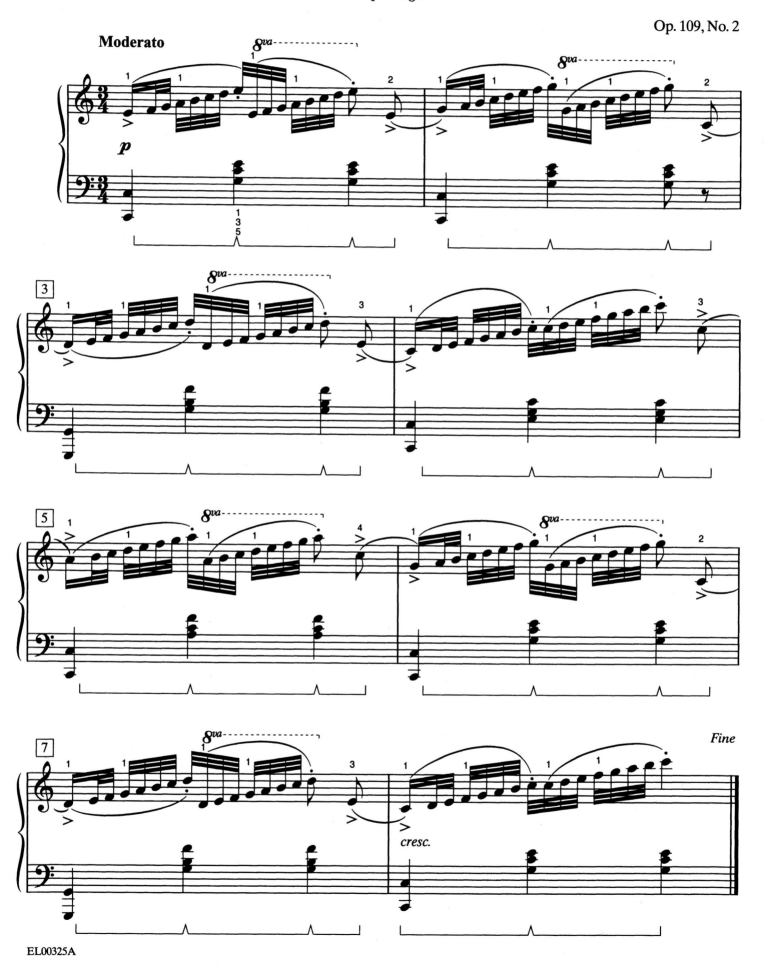

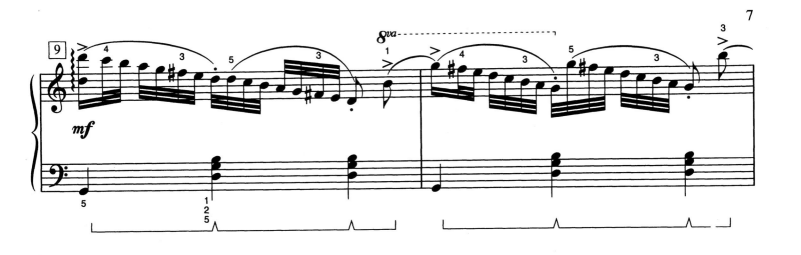

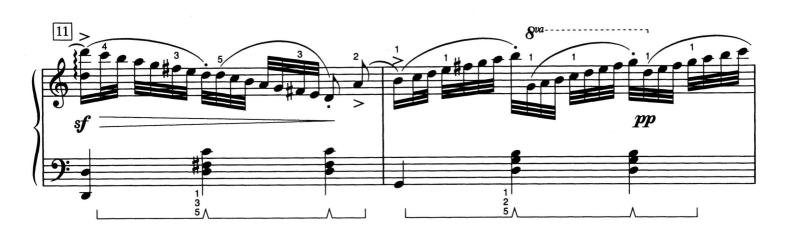

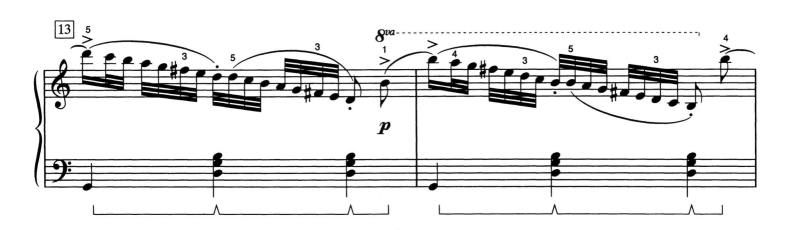

THE GYPSIES
Staccato study in a minor key

Op. 109, No. 4

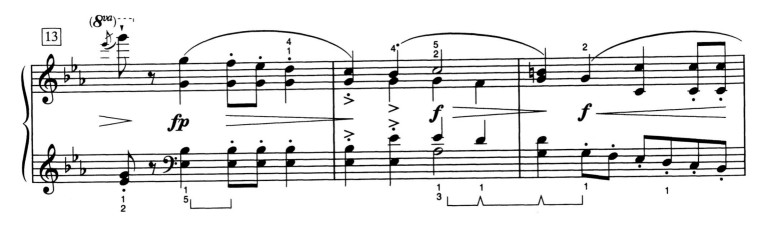

EL00325A

SPRINGTIME
Broken chord study

Op. 109, No. 5

Andante grazioso

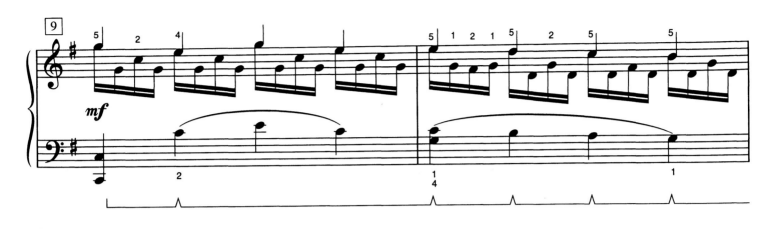

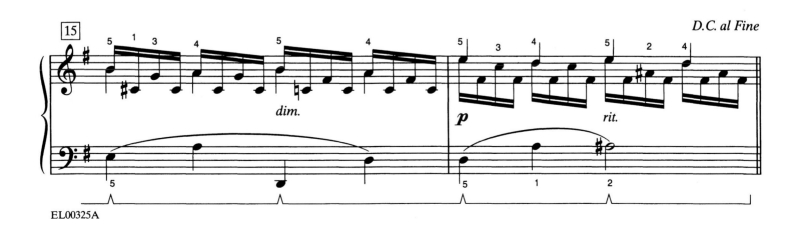

JUMPING ROPE
Double note and wrist staccato study

Op. 109, No. 6

Allegretto

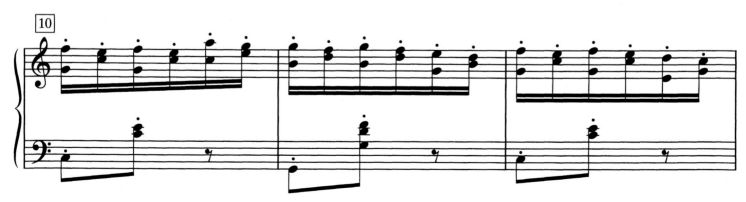

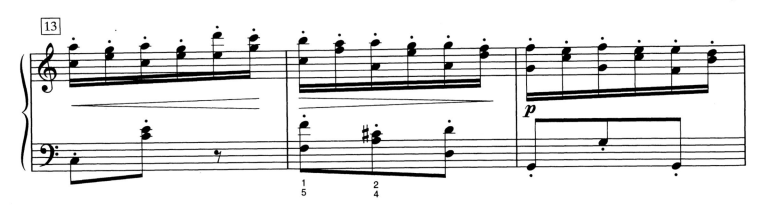

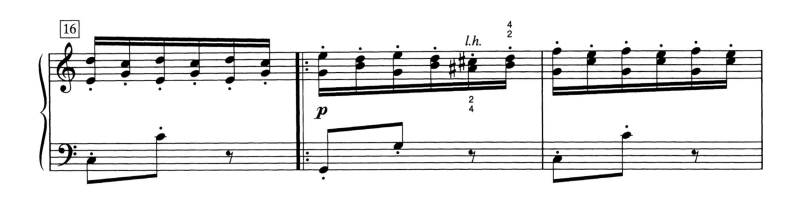

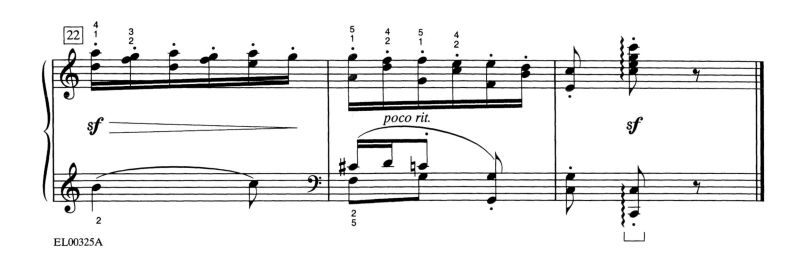

SAILING
Study in legato, shading, tone, and interpretation

Op. 109, No. 7

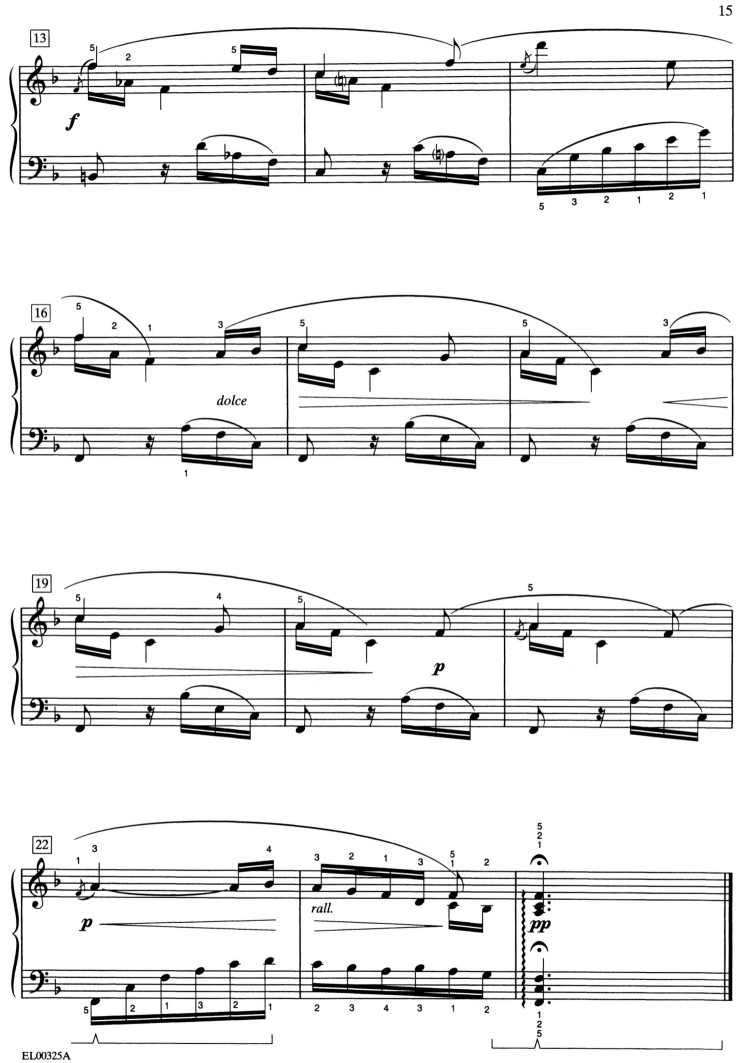

THE RESTLESS MOLECULE

Interlocking hand legato

Op. 109, No. 8

Allegro vivace

CHURCH BELLS

Cross-hand study

Op. 109, No. 9

SNOW FLURRIES*

Velocity study

Op. 109, No. 10

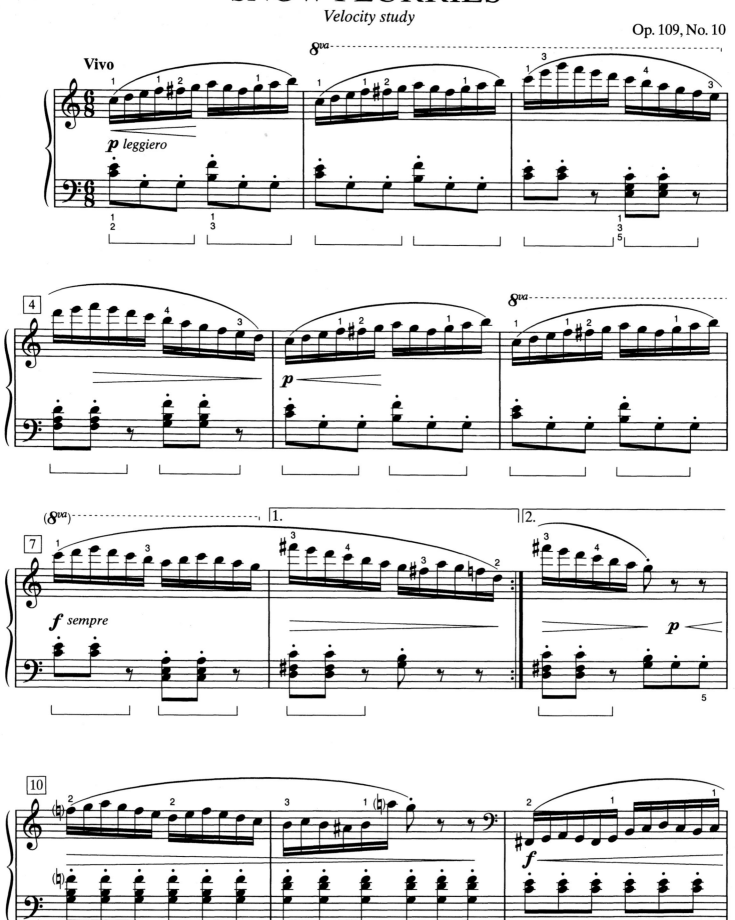

*Originally titled "Geschwindigkeit" indicating high speed or velocity, this piece is presented in its original form with a few helpful
  fingerings and pedal markings added.

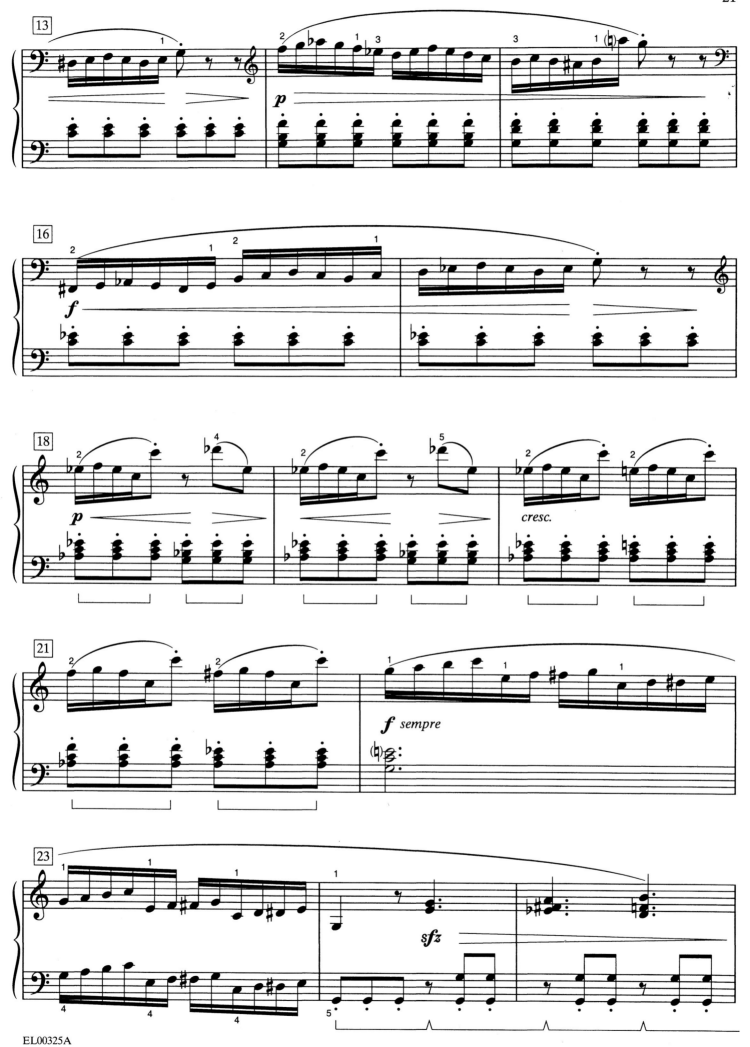

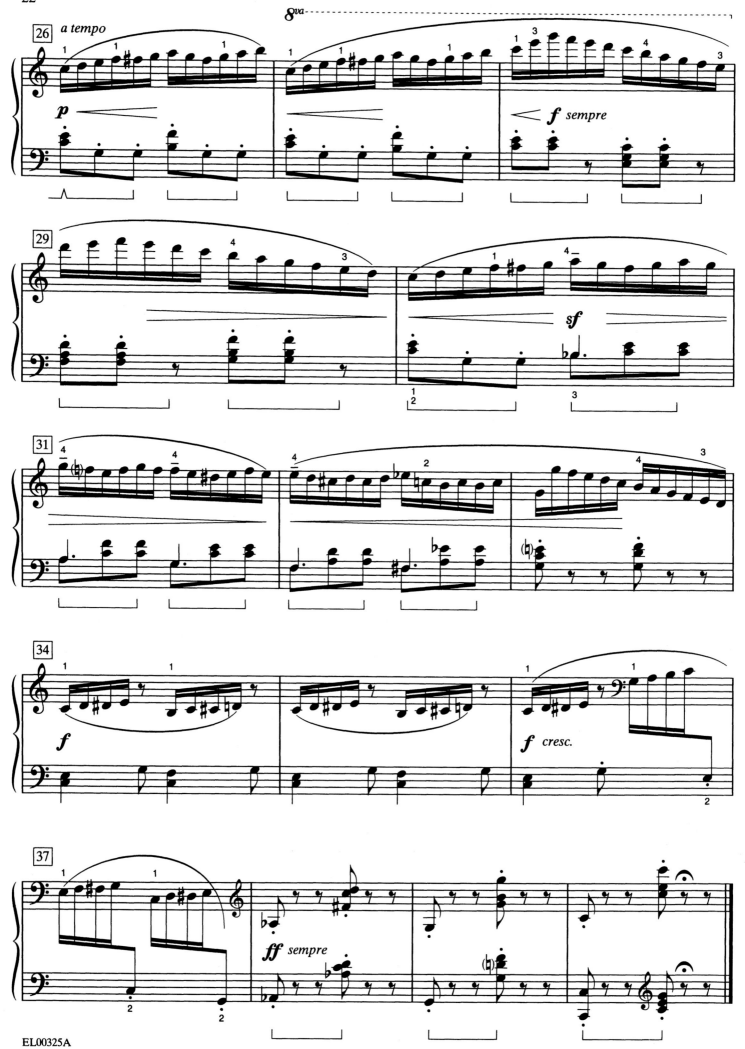

DOG TROT
Broken octave study

*Op. 109, No. 12

*This piece is presented in its original form.

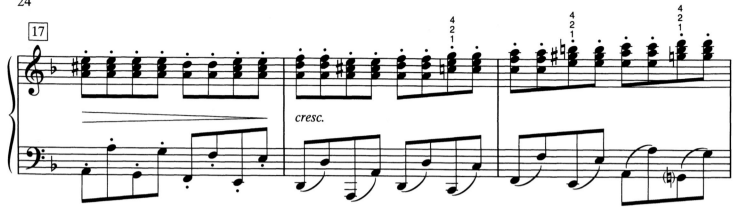

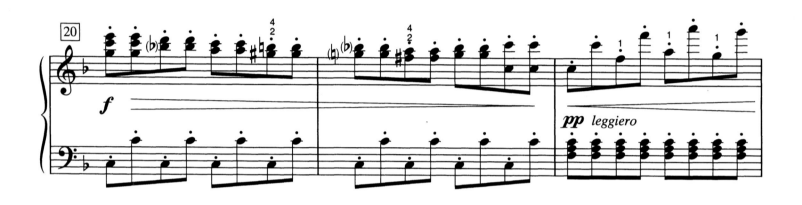

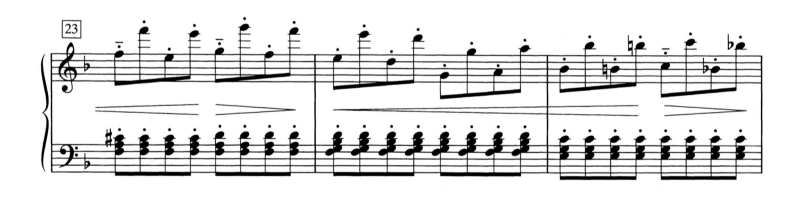

PATIO DANCING

Grace note study

Allegretto grazioso

Op. 109, No. 11

THUNDER STORM

Dynamic shading and interpretation

Op. 109, No. 13

THE GONDOLIER'S SONG

Left-hand broken chords

Op. 109, No. 14

ACROBATIC DANCER

Attack and release of small groups

Op. 109, No. 15

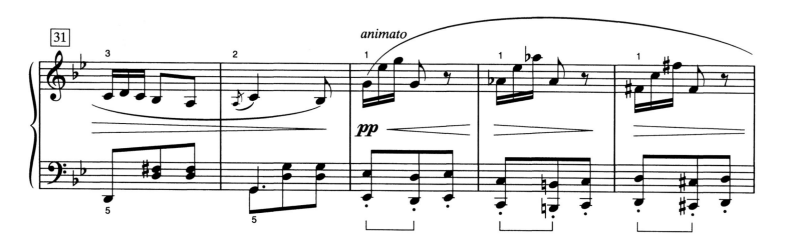

UNDERTOW
Left-hand melody

Op. 109, No. 16

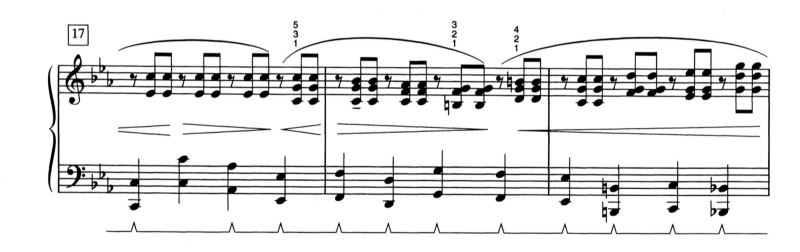

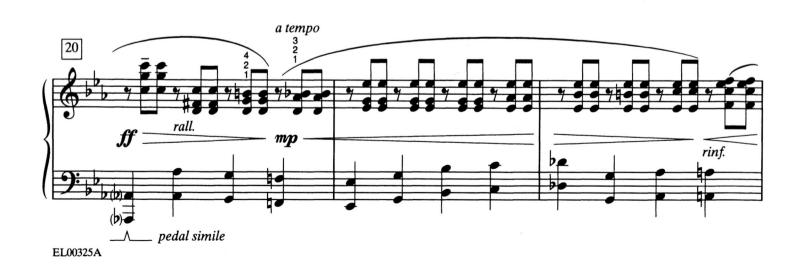

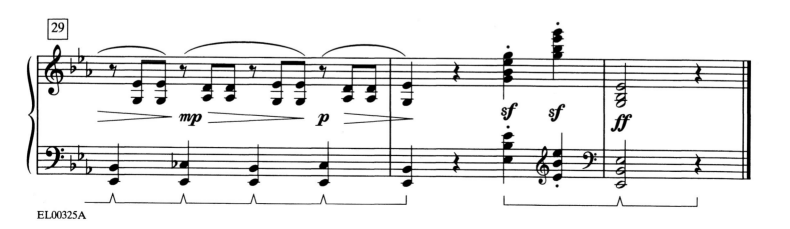

MARCH

Full chords with rhythmic precision

Op. 109, No. 17

THE SPINNING TOP

Study in right-hand passage playing

Op. 109, No. 18

*Burgmüller's original manuscript uses triplet sixteenths. Mr. Schaum indicates eighth note triplets for greater clarity and ease in reading the score.

EL00325A